Flight to Freedom

World War II through the eyes of a child

The Story of Philomena Keller Baker

by Kathryn Olmstead and Philomena Baker

This is Philomena Baker's story as told to Kathryn Olmstead and reinforced by the recollections of German relatives who helped keep these memories alive in the family by retelling them over the years. The authors are mindful that the historical context for this story is far more complex than this memoir presents. While significant effort has been made to provide some historical background, this is a personal story of one family's experience, one piece of a much larger picture.

Flight to Freedom
©2013 Kathryn Olmstead and Philomena Baker
ISBN 978-1-938883-15-6

Designed and Produced by
Maine Authors Publishing
558 Main Street, Rockland, Maine 04841
www.maineauthorspublishing.com

This book is dedicated to

Philomene Keller

*whose wisdom, courage and compassion
it commemorates*

A Prophecy

The old gypsy ducked behind the high brick wall surrounding a home in Selz when she realized she had been seen. She did not want to cause trouble for the young girl who had spied her through the lattice opening in the gate as she crossed her yard. Beggars and gypsies were attracted to German colonies in Ukraine where hard-working, well-to-do people were known to be generous. Villagers in Selz had been ordered not to feed them when they came into town looking for food.

Nevertheless, young Philomene approached the gypsy and assured her she need not be fearful. "Stay right here," she said with her hands as well as her voice, for she recognized the old woman was deaf and mute. She returned to her house where freshly baked loaves of bread were cooling in the kitchen. Casually, she slipped a loaf under her apron and returned to the yard where the gypsy waited outside the gate.

The old woman knew Philomene had taken a risk by giving her food and said thank you with a blessing. She wanted the young girl to know that God saw her goodness and would reward her for her kindness. She raised her right hand and pointed to the sky, then to Philomene's heart. Then she raised both hands, made a rocking motion with her arms and pointed to Philomene's heart once more. Her message: Philomene would have one child. Both she and her child would be blessed and guided through their long lives.

Philomene never forgot the gypsy's blessing. It foretold the life that lay ahead of her.

Contents

A Prophecy vii

Preface xi

Historical Perspective xiv

Part I: ODESSA

1 • Philomene 3

2 • Philomena 15

Part II: FLIGHT

3 • The Train Ride 31

4 • German-Occupied Poland 37

5 • Potsdam 41

Part III: THE LONG WALK

6 • To the Elbe River 47

7 • American-Occupied Germany 55

Part IV: FREEDOM

8 • Bavaria 63

9 • Maine 75

Epilogue • The Race Walker 83

Afterword • How life evolved 87

Sources 90

Acknowledgements 92

About The Authors 93

Preface

Philomena Keller Baker hesitates when asked where she is from. The inclination to be vague about her origins lingered long after World War II, when telling the truth would have been dangerous. Once she accepted that it was safe to share, her stories began to flow, running this way and that way in a multitude of remarkable experiences.

"So many people expressed an interest in the story of my flight from Russia as a 10-year-old during World War II, I decided to record my recollections," said the Bangor Reiki master, well known throughout New England for her long career as a professional portrait photographer. "Mine is a story that ends in Maine where I am reminded daily of the blessings of freedom and peace."

It is a story that begins in Odessa—a tale of a 40-year-old mother, Philomene, and her young daughter, Philomena, set in the midst of World War II. It is also the story of two sisters, Philomene and Julia, both widowed by the war, determined to shepherd their children to safety and to shield them from the violence surrounding them. And it is a story of cousins, who in their 70s and 80s continued to marvel at the extraordinary circumstances that kept them connected through their remarkable flight to freedom.

It is not an easy story to assemble. Philomena was 9 years old in 1944 when she and her mother boarded a freight car attached to a German army hospital train in Odessa, Ukraine, and became part of a massive westward migration of German civilians fleeing the Red Army. Dropped in Poland with new German citizenship papers, she and her mother walked most of the way to American-occupied Germany, crossing the Elbe River just as the Germans surrendered to the Allies in May 1945.

Philomena's memories are vivid snapshots of scenes and episodes with indistinct connections among them. "I feel like a computer," she said. "It is all stored, and I am retrieving it."

So successful were the efforts of Philomene and Julia to protect their children from the dangers propelling their escape that Philomena struggled to reconstruct the events that led them to safety. Periodically, she called her older cousins in Germany to piece together details. As they blended their memories, they recognized their place in history and the good fortune that kept them alive to tell their story.

Philomena had been married two years before her husband learned she was born in Russia. They had met in Germany long after she had begun to identify more with her mother's German ancestry than with her father's roots in Ukraine. The fear that she might be captured and returned to Russia prevented her from talking much about her childhood, even after she had moved to the United States.

Besides, things got busy after John A. Baker brought his bride home to Fort Kent, Maine, in 1959. Two years later they were the parents of two daughters, and by 1963 Philomena had opened a photography studio on Main Street, launching a 40-year career in portrait and commercial photography. The story of her year as a refugee, walking with her mother most of the way from Poland to western Germany, just got buried beneath her work as a professional photographer, wife and mother. It began to resurface during a ride from Portland to Bangor, Maine, when Dr. Zev Myerowitz, son of her second husband, Dr. Moshe Myerowitz, asked her about her origins.

"It just started pouring out," she said. "I talked the entire way from Portland to Bangor and he didn't say a word." But Dr. Zev did show interest. So did others with whom she began to share pieces of the odyssey. They said she should write a book.

"But I'm not a writer," she lamented.

Years passed. Motivation intensified.

I met Philomena through a former student who was helping her improve her computer skills. Philomena had written a short autobiographical essay to be submitted for a radio broadcast competition of personal stories. She was given a time limit for the radio script. My student guessed correctly that Philomena had much more to tell. She urged Philomena not to wait until she had mastered the computer to record her story and suggested I contact her. We met for the first time at Bagel Central in Bangor in 2009.

"You will recognize me by my bright red hair," she said. Oh yes—I could not miss the lady beside the window with hair the color of saffron. She presented me with two and a half pages of memories handwritten in pencil and titled "The War, seen through a child's eyes." The interviews began.

The meeting in the bagel shop led to many meetings, some in the second floor library between Java Joe's and BookMarc's in downtown Bangor. Meetings led to manuscripts, version after version, as she added details to the story and I filled composition books with notes.

Then I asked if she had any old photographs and we ended up in her Bangor home with photos dating from the late 1800s to the present spread across her dining table. They portray Philomena's father, who disappeared into the Soviet Army, and two uncles who were taken to Siberia, never to return. Generations of her family gaze from a 1908 photo of a 50th anniversary celebration that shows the prosperity of Germans who cultivated land in Ukraine until communism erased private ownership. These and many other archival photos made the perilous journey with Philomena and her mother from Odessa to Germany in 1944 and 1945. They appear in this book because Philomena's mother valued and protected them.

It is not surprising that Philomena became a photographer. And it is not surprising that, in her 50s, she became a champion racewalker. After all, she had walked halfway across Germany at the age of 10.

Kathryn Olmstead
September 2012

Historical Perspective
Events relevant to Philomena's Story
Events mentioned in the story are in bold.

1939

Aug. 23 –   Soviet Union signs non-aggression pact with Germany

Sept. 1 –   Germany invades Poland

Sept. 17 –   Soviet Union invades Poland

1941

June 22 –   **Germany invades Soviet Union**

Sept. 8 –   Germans lay siege to Leningrad

Sept. 19 –   Germans capture Kiev

Nov. 8 –   Germans move into Crimea

Dec. 5 –   German drive on Moscow halted

Dec. 11 –   Germany and Italy declare war on U.S.

1942

June 25 –   German troops take Kharkov on Eastern front

July 1 –   Germans secure Sevastopol in the Crimea

Aug. 9 –   Germans capture oil fields in the Caucasus

Aug. 12 –   Churchill, Stalin, U.S. and French representatives meet in Moscow

Sept.-Dec. –   Germans reach Stalingrad, Soviets hold city

1943

Jan. 14 –	Roosevelt and Churchill meet at Casablanca
Aug. 5 –	Soviets recapture Orel and Belgorod in drive to **Dnieper River, the last German defensive line in Soviet territory**
Sept. 22 –	Soviets secure first bridgehead across the Dnieper
Nov. 7 –	**German defenses on Dnieper begin to crumble**

1944

Jan. 27 –	Soviets defeat Germans at Leningrad
April 10 –	**Soviets recapture Odessa in Ukraine**
April 15 –	Soviets take Tarnopol in Ukraine
May 9 –	Soviets recapture Sevastopol

1945

Jan. 19 –	Germany in full retreat on Eastern front
April 12 –	Roosevelt dies
April 16 –	Soviets begin all-out attack on Berlin
April 23 –	**Soviets enter Berlin**
April 25 –	**U.S. and Soviet forces meet at Elbe River**
April 30 –	Hitler commits suicide in Berlin
May 1 –	Berlin surrenders to occupying Soviet forces
May 7 –	**Germany formally surrenders**
June 5 –	**Allies divide Germany into four occupation zones controlled by Russia, France, Britain and the United States.**

SOURCE *WWII: Time-Life Books History of the Second World War*, by the editors of Time-Life Books, Foreword by Eric Sevareid, Prentice-Hall Press, New York, 1989

Part I

ODESSA

1
Philomene

Philomena Baker's mother
She was Russian, but she was really German

Philomene Keller and the two brothers she never saw again after they
parted in Odessa where they had this picture taken when they met
by chance in the 1920s.

Philomene thought she heard heavy footsteps on the winding
stair leading to the room she rented in a farmhouse near Odessa.
She was home from school with a high fever. She could not teach
today. She couldn't even rise from her bed.

Did she hear knocks on the door? Or was she dreaming? She
was so sick, she wasn't sure. She fell back to sleep. It was late afternoon when she finally awoke to the voice of her landlady outside
the door.

"Philomene! Philomene! Are you in there?"

Still delirious, she unlocked the door.

"Philomene, the police were here looking for you today, the military police. I told them you weren't here. I told them you were at school teaching."

It was not a dream—the footsteps, the knocks. Philomene had known this day would come, as it had come for her brothers and her mother. Unlike her relatives, Philomene spoke perfect Russian. She taught Russian children in an elementary school. Her fluency had been a passport to opportunity—an education, a job as a teacher—advantages unavailable to family members who spoke primarily German.

But like them, she was German. And it was not good to be German in Odessa in the 1920s.

Ancestry

When she ascended to the throne of the Russian Empire in 1762, Catherine II, also known as Catherine the Great, was determined to convert the lowland plains and plateaus of Ukraine into productive farmlands. Born a German, Catherine knew Germans were skilled in agriculture and husbandry. She advertised in German newspapers offering attractive terms for settlers to come and cultivate the vast lands north of the Black Sea. Thousands responded by moving in large groups toward Russia. Those who endured the long eastward journey eventually crossed the Carpathian Mountains and settled in the land promised by Catherine the Great.

Many of those who accepted the offer were from Alsace-Lorraine, the long-disputed region on the borders of France and Germany. After generations of wars, life in a new territory must have appealed to German farmers who formed lovely colonies along the Dnieper River, near the port city of Odessa, where they had easy access to water for their farms and homes. By 1897, more than a half million Germans and Mennonites had migrated

Above: "Beautiful Selz," the German village on the Dnieper River in Ukraine, home of Keller ancestors, named after a place in Alsace-Lorraine from which the colony's original settlers came in the 1800s.

Right: Philomene Keller's Aunt Gertrude who ran the orphanage where Philomeme stayed as a child and learned to speak the Russian language.

Below: The 1908 50th wedding anniversary celebration for Marianne and Johannes Keller (center), reflecting the prosperity of the people in the German colonies along the Dnieper River. Adam and Theresa Keller (far right) are the parents of Philomene, who is sitting on the lap of her favorite Aunt Gertrude. Theresa is holding her son, Rudolf.

to the Dnieper region of Ukraine. They had their own German language schools and churches, self government, tax privileges and, until 1871, exemption from military service, writes Paul Robert Magosci in *Ukraine: An Illustrated History* (2007).

Philomene Keller was born into one of these German communities, Selz, in 1903, the youngest girl among eight children. The memories of her youth now live in the stories of her daughter, Philomena Keller Baker.

The village of Selz was named after the place in Alsace-Lorraine from which Philomene's ancestors had migrated. The Dnieper River ran behind the buildings on one side of a wide road through the village. On the opposite side, vineyards stretched out behind the buildings as far as the eye could see, and farther. Homes had gardens behind them and brick walls in front.

Philomene's relatives prospered in Selz, cultivating their land into productive vineyards, selling and bartering fine wines in the city. Barrels of wine were like liquid money. They were self-sufficient, feeding themselves and their animals with the bounty of their gardens and fields. They also planted walnut trees. They were a hardworking, proud and religious people. Many lived to be older than 100, enjoying healthy, happy lives, working on the farms into old age. Keller family records show that one grandfather lived to be 108, a grandmother 105 and another relative 103.

Youth

The fields on the German farms were so large that when the workers progressed to the outer reaches during planting and harvest they would camp out instead of returning home at the end of a day. They worked into the night and slept on the ground. Philomena asked her mother how they stayed warm. "Oh, the tall grass was warmed by the sun during the day," she replied. "It was soft and we were so tired. We slept." When food and water ran low, workers would return to the village with a team of horses and bring back food and supplies the next morning.

"My mother had the responsibility of taking a horse-drawn carriage to get supplies, bread, water and food. People in the fields knew when she was returning before they saw her because they could hear her singing. My mother had a beautiful voice. She sang second soprano in the church choir in Selz. Her sister Regina sang soprano and they were well-known for the beautiful harmony of their voices."

Before Philomene was old enough to work in the fields with her parents and older siblings, she stayed with her mother's sister, Gertrude, who operated an orphanage for German and Russian children. She and her Aunt Gertrude grew very close. Her schooling at the orphanage included the Russian language. Philomene became as fluent in Russian as she was in the German spoken in her home. As she grew older, she could pass for a native of either country. Eventually she was able to become a schoolteacher in a Russian elementary school. Years later, during World War II, her bilingual fluency would enable her to save her whole family.

Born during the reign of Tsar Nicholas II, Philomene grew up in a period of political turmoil. She was a teenager in 1918 when Nicholas and his family were executed in July and when, on October 25, the Bolsheviks, led by Vladimir Lenin, seized power in an assault on the Winter Palace. She was in her late teens when Lenin's policies caused a two-year famine that claimed the lives of 1.5 to 2 million people in Soviet Ukraine.

She was 21 in 1924 when Lenin died and Josef Stalin began his struggle to control the Communist Party. She would witness the effects of Stalin's rule as private ownership of land dissolved and those who were well-to-do or who resisted collectivism were captured and sent to work camps in Siberia. The good fortune of the German farmers ended with the rise of Stalin.

Well-to-do peasants, called kulaks, were the first to go. An estimated 250,000 kulaks and their families were deported from Soviet Ukraine to the central and eastern regions of the Soviet Union between January and March of 1930, according to Margosci. "During the forced transports to these remote and inhospitable regions, thousands died along the way or soon after arrival," he writes, adding that another million peasant workers were deported to the east in 1931 and 1932.

Communism

When the Russian communists moved to reclaim the land that had been given to the Germans, farm families were forced to escape into the city of Odessa. The happy country life of Philomene's youth was eclipsed by the shadow of fear. German men lived in constant fear of execution or capture and relocation to labor camps where they worked for nothing, like slaves, in forests and mines.

Philomena relates her mother's memories:

"When the communists came to power in the early 20th century, they began persecuting the German settlers because they had so much abundance and food and took care of themselves well, while the communist regime could not provide for their own people and many started to die of hunger.

"When German people saw communist police on the streets, word would spread quickly in the community so the men could hide. One of my mother's brothers hid from the communists in a chimney. One hid under a haystack, and another brother escaped through the back yard. He broke off a big branch from a tree and hid behind it, slowly removing himself from the yard to safety. They moved frequently and often did not know where family members were.

"One day my mother saw one of her brothers on the street in Odessa. She called to him and they were chatting when they saw another brother. It was such a coincidence, they decided to have their picture taken together. That was the last time she saw either of her brothers."

Philomena's uncles simply disappeared, as did millions of others at that time. One or two came back. One of her mother's brothers returned from Siberia marked by the emotional effects of water torture. He was never the same.

"The regime began to torture the German people because they were prosperous," Philomena explained. "They came and raved at them in their villages. They collected men and brought them to the outskirts of the village in the middle of the night or in the early mornings. They forced them to dig a deep hole and stand around it. While the women and children watched, they shot the men into the grave.

"The police were assigned to go from house to house to look for younger German men. They took them to Siberia, where, in deep snow and freezing weather, they had to build cabins to live in and were subjected to water-drop torture.

"My mother's sister, Maria, was expecting a child when she heard that communists were looking for men in Selz to send to Siberia. When the uniformed police arrived at the house asking for her husband, he was hiding in a closet."

The men entered the home and began their search. "He's not here," Maria insisted. They opened one closet door after another. Maria braced her back against the door concealing her husband. When she refused them access to that closet, they shot her in the hip, barely missing the baby in her womb. They took her husband away and left her bleeding on the floor where her neighbors found her when they came to the rescue.

"I always remember my Aunt Maria as a severely limping woman, and learned only recently why," Philomena said. "The child she bore was a boy they named Peter. He was born 90 percent blind, seeing only shadows, as a result of his mother's injuries. He still lives on his own in Germany."

The Rescue
The story of how Philomene rescued her mother from the communists has been told among Philomena's German relatives for decades.

Philomene at the age she might have been when she rescued her mother from the Russian communists.

"My grandmother, Theresa, was still living on the family farm in Selz when the Russian communists came for her," Philomena said. "She had been ill and was bedridden. My mother told me the communists carried her mother from her room, mattress and all, and threw her into the back of a horse-drawn wagon. They took her to Siberia, a long distance from the village."

Philomene was still young and unmarried, teaching Russian children in the vicinity of Odessa. Unlike her older sister, Julia, she did not have the responsibilities of family. She could act on her outrage—she could devise and execute a plan to rescue her mother during her summer break from teaching school.

She planned every detail. When she had everything she needed, she boarded the train for Siberia. Among her provisions for the trip were a few packs of cigarettes and some apples. Food was scarce and cigarettes were a precious luxury. These items could be useful in gaining access to her mother. A modest young woman, she dressed so as not to attract attention, but she could not hide her beauty.

"My mother found the place out in the country where her mother was being held. It was a huge compound constructed like a prison. The inhabitants slept on the floor and had no water. Twice a day they were led to a stream behind the building where they were allowed to get water and wash.

"The building was surrounded by a wall. My mother could see the heads of the Russian guards and climbed up the wall enough to get their attention. Using the cigarettes as a bribe and her fluency in Russian, she engaged the guards in conversation and found out when the people in the compound would be making their next trip to the river."

Philomene must have withdrawn to a spot where she would be able to see the procession. When the gates opened and people moved toward the river, she was part of the shrubbery. She made some signal that enabled her mother to identify her and to slip into the bushes with her. They stood silently, gradually inching away. When the group returned to the compound, they fled to the station to await the next train to Odessa.

"My mother did not want her mother to speak to the conductor because her broken Russian would reveal that she was German. 'Pretend you are sleeping,' she told her. The conductor was a young man. He took my mother's ticket and then asked about the woman huddled next to the window. 'She's just an old babushka. Let her sleep,' she said. She took a bite out of one of her precious apples, proving it was safe to eat, then stuffed it into the mouth of the surprised conductor. 'Here, have an apple.' He moved on without asking for my grandmother's ticket. My mother had successfully distracted him."

When they arrived in Odessa, Philomene took her mother to live with her oldest sister, Julia, and her family and returned to her rented room near the elementary school. But she was not out of harm's way. Word had gotten around that she was German.

Wasja

Had Philomene not been ill the day the Russian police knocked on the door of her upstairs room, she might have fallen victim to

Philomene and her brother Andreas
(1920s?).

Wasja Semenenko in the 1930s(?).

Russian elementary school students in Odessa surround their two teachers,
Philomene on left.

Philomene Keller Semenenka when she was pregnant with Philomena (1933 to 1934).

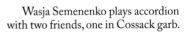

Wasja Semenenko plays accordion with two friends, one in Cossack garb.

Philomena's Aunt Maria and her son, Peter, who was born nearly blind because she was shot in the hip when she was pregnant with him.

the kind of treatment her mother had endured. She was fortunate to have a compassionate landlady who continued to protect her each time the communists returned to the farmhouse looking for her.

Nevertheless, she did not feel safe. The corn in a nearby field had grown high enough to conceal her and she decided to hide in that field, returning from time to time for information and food from her landlady.

She had been hiding 10 days when she was discovered by a young man who lived with his parents in a house next to the field. His name was Wasja Semenenko. He was tall and good-looking with curly hair. He persuaded Philomene to come home with him and stay with his family.

It is not known how long she remained with the Semenenkos. It is known that she stayed long enough to fall in love. Eventually Wasja and Philomene were married. Her new surname concealed her German identity. She was now Philomene Semenenka,* but Wasja called her Marousia, Russian for Mary. Their daughter Philomena was born June 6, 1934, in Odessa.

* "a" denotes the feminine

2
Philomena

A happy childhood

Philomene and her daughter Philomena (circa. 1938).

Philomena's name reflected her dual heritage as the only child of a German mother and a Russian father: Philomena, after her mother, Philomene; Wasjelevna, a feminization of her father's first name, as was customary in Russia—Philomena Wasjelevna Semenenka.

Philomene (Marousia) was 30 when her daughter Philomena was born in 1934. It was a time in Russia when millions were dying under the rule of Josef Stalin. Deportation of well-to-do peasant farmers combined with forced grain requisitioning caused a drop in the harvests of 1931 and 1932. Famine broke out in 1932.

Famine and Illness

"By the winter of 1933, widespread starvation raged throughout most of the countryside," writes Paul Magocsi. "Estimates for 1933 alone range from 4.5 to 5 million deaths, and as many as 10 million deaths during the rest of the decade are attributed to what became known as the Great Famine." Since the Soviet government at the time and for the next half century denied that a famine ever existed, the number of fatalities has been determined through demographic studies. Magocsi reports that the largest decline in Soviet Ukraine's population occurred from 1931 through 1934, when the republic suffered a net loss of 4.1 million people.

"My mother told me that when she was pregnant with me, people were dying of starvation in Odessa. She said it would break her heart to see people dying and already dead on the street when she was walking to work."

Philomena's mother also had a personal concern. Malaria had spread to Ukraine from other countries around the Black Sea and Wasja Semenenko was one of many in the region to be stricken. There were no medications, and doctors believed the disease would cause birth defects in children if a parent was infected.

"My father suffered from malaria for a long time. When he and my mother were expecting me he wanted her to see the doctor, so she did. The doctor verified she was expecting, but suggested she have an abortion because of my father's illness. My mother had a firm religious background and refused to do that. 'I will let God make that decision,' she said. She was convinced that if God did not want me to be born, that would be His decision. And so she carried me and I was born in a Russian hospital on June 6, 1934, in the beautiful city of Odessa.

"My mother was Catholic, but not fanatical. When she could go to church, she did. When she couldn't, she did not feel guilty. She was connected to a higher power and believed in its guidance. She trusted in God's presence and accepted what life gave her. She did not want to meddle in God's work. If it was meant to be,

Above: Philomena (center) with her father, when he was suffering from malaria, and her cousin Viktoria (late 1930s).

Left: "I was very sick in this photograph. My mother stopped to have my picture taken on the way to the hospital."

Below: Philomena (center) with her mother and a girlfriend beside the Black Sea where they were swimming (1939).

God would provide. She always said, 'We need to adapt ourselves to the situation.' Her faith guided her in our long journey to freedom. She believed that every step of the way was prepared for us."

When Philomena was a baby, her mother took her to an old woman who was known to be a healer.

"Doctors and hospitals were rare and crowded. I was very ill—limp and not eating. The old woman took me in her arms and held me in prayer. Then she gave me back to my mother and went into another room where she prayed before a sacred icon. As my mother waited, she heard an explosion. The old woman had thrown an egg wrapped in thread into the fireplace and was very pleased when it exploded. She told my mother the explosion was a sign that I would be well.

"As soon as we were home, I asked for 'Borshiko.' I wanted borscht, a popular Russian stew with cabbage, beets, potatoes, other vegetables and a well-cooked beef bone. My mother was surprised. Those were my first words since I had become ill."

Philomena remembers her mother as a gentle and calm, yet strong woman, thinking in ways we think today. "She taught me not to be fearful, but to trust faith and follow its guidance. She was gentle, self-controlled, intelligent and always cheerful. She never showed anger, but if anyone tried to hurt me as a child, she would have strong words with them. She had a lot of wisdom.

"There were many beggars on the streets of Odessa, some who pretended they couldn't walk. We didn't have much to give, but she would always give me some money to give to the poor. In this way she taught me compassion for others, and I am grateful for this. My mother would not hurt or insult anyone."

Looking back, Philomena can see how her mother prepared her for the rigors they would face together. "We would imitate circus performers. I remember climbing trees and hanging from branches by my knees. I was good at acrobatics and she encouraged me. Our agility would prove to be a life-saving skill for us."

Wasja Semenenko in the 1930s, proud owner of a truck he used for his work in Odessa.

Extended Family

By the time Philomena was 6, her father had disappeared. Even though he had malaria, he was drafted into the Soviet Army during World War II before the Germans occupied Odessa. Like many others, he just never came home.

"The military felt no obligation to the families of soldiers. They made no effort to contact family members when a soldier died or was missing. My mother searched for my father, but was never certain what became of him.

"I remember my father mostly through hearsay. My cousin, Viktoria, is eight years older than I, and she loves to tell me how my father would collect the children for rides in the back of his truck, the first and only truck in the community.

"We had a great time riding in the back of the truck, holding onto the sides," Viktoria told Philomena. "We laughed and squealed when we saw the trees fly by." But then Viktoria's face would turn thoughtful and concerned when she remembered the truck crossing a narrow bridge with no railings on a pair of planks set the width of the tires. But he always brought them home safely. He would laugh and joke with the children, delighted to make them happy.

Viktoria's mother, Julia, also lost her husband to the war. Johannes Hartmann Sr. had been home on leave. After he returned to his company, he was never seen again. Julia cherished the picture of her husband wearing his officer's uniform. "They always believed that he would return," Philomena said.

Left with five children, Julia was very close to her youngest sister, Philomene. Their children were like siblings. Julia's youngest son, Johnannes Jr., was a year younger than Philomena. The others were Angelika (the oldest girl), Josef (the oldest boy), Viktoria and Alfred.

"Josef was a very gifted young man. I knew him best when he was about 16," Philomena recalled. "He never had a piano lesson, but when he heard a melody, he could sit down and play it. He would play Russian songs, German songs and any melody that he would hear. We had no piano where we lived, but someone gave the family a piano so Josef could play."

Philomene, her sister Julia and their children lived on Srednia, a main street in Odessa, before the city was occupied by the German army. Viktoria was like a mother to the younger children, hurrying home from school to care for them while the two mothers and her older sister, Angelika, were still at work.

"When Viktoria came home she put the house in order and made sure everyone behaved themselves until my mother and Aunt Julia came home to prepare our dinners, which were always quite sparse.

"Viktoria stayed with me during her summer vacation. One time she decided to go swimming in the Black Sea with two of her friends. She was not supposed to do that when she was caring for me. You had to go down over steep rocks to get to the small beach that came and went with the tides. Viktoria and her friends told me to stay on the shore while they went swimming into the waves of the Black Sea. However, I decided to go into the water. A wave came, and I disappeared. Viktoria turned back to look for me and I was gone. Frantic, she and her friends swam back

Johannes Hartmann Sr., husband of Philomene's sister, Julia, in his Russian army uniform and winter outfit (1916-1917).

Johannes Hartmann Sr., wounded, with doctor and two officers (1916-17).

and found me unconscious on the beach. They picked me up by the legs, head down, and slapped me on the back to eliminate the water from my lungs and to revive me. They succeeded, but I had come close to death."

Childplay

Philomena's memories of her childhood in Odessa are filled with images of children playing together. Her cousin Alfred used to carry her on his shoulders, and they still talk about the day he stumbled and she tumbled over his head, suffering only minor injuries when she hit the stony ground.

"We lived in the city next to a park and most of my friends were my age. We chased each other and used large old trees to play hide and seek. We didn't have toys. We had to make up our own games. It was a simple life, fun life, carefree for us—probably not so carefree for the grown-ups who had to work to sustain our life, hoping each day that we all would remain unharmed.

"At harvest time my uncle would come into Odessa from our German village on a wagon pulled by horses. He would stop by our door with loads of fruits and vegetables for the rest of the season, but the most exciting were the grapes that filled half of his wagon. We climbed on top of the wagon and grabbed as many grapes as we could fit into our pockets. Our uncle warned us to be gentle around the pockets, not to squash the grapes. For the rest of the week, we ate grapes. We didn't mind. We loved it."

At that time, Philomena's mother worked in the kitchen of a sanitarium for children with tuberculosis and other illnesses. In a photo of the kitchen staff, Philomene and her co-workers carry gas masks on straps over their shoulders in case of an attack. The hospital grew all its own food and provided housing for its workers.

"We lived in a small brick house with a walkway to the hospital on one side and another walkway to the Black Sea on the other side. My mother preferred a job involving food, which allowed

Philomene (front left) worked in the kitchen of a sanitarium for children with tuberculosis and other diseases during the 1930s in Odessa.

Philomene (right) and two co-workers in the kitchen of the children's hospital with gas masks strapped over their shoulders in case of an attack.

her to help feed her family during war time.

"When I was 5 years old, my friends and I liked to play around a fountain near the sanitarium where my mother worked. We loved to throw rocks into the water to see them splash. One afternoon a rock hit me on the left side of my head and rendered me unconscious. When I awoke, all my friends were gone. I stood up and tried to walk toward the building where my mother worked. She saw me through the window weaving back and forth and came rushing out. The lump on my head was swelling.

"She took me home and applied compresses of denatured alcohol through the night—a home remedy known to keep the blood from clotting and to keep the swelling down. She knew it was important that I not fall asleep, so she stayed awake with me through the night. The next morning, as soon as the streetcars started to move, she took me to the city hospital where they drained the wound, filling a kidney-shaped pan with the remaining accumulated blood. My mother stopped to have my picture taken at a photographic studio on the way to the hospital to have a record of this unfortunate event in my life."

German Occupation

Philomena didn't want to speak German. It was OK when she was visiting her mother's relatives in the country who spoke German, but she had always spoken Russian at home in Odessa. All her friends spoke Russian. Her mother loved the Russian language and spoke it beautifully. But she started introducing German into their conversations, even at home, suggesting Philomena say things in German instead of Russian.

Things had started to change after her father was drafted into the Soviet army and did not return. They kept hoping to hear from him, but there was no word. Time passed.

Then the German army occupied Odessa on June 22, 1941. Philomena was 7. Homes in the best section of Odessa became housing for German families. The brick structures opened onto

Children playing in the courtyard of Deutsche Haus in Odessa.

landscaped courtyards where the children played. Julia, Philomene, their children and an older aunt, also named Julia, lived in one of these buildings, called the Deutsche Haus (German House).

"Each of our two families had their own private space for sleeping and eating that opened onto a larger dining room with a long table. My mother and I had a small room off the large room with a wood cookstove and a small dining table."

Philomene made frequent trips on the streetcar from this home to a farm outside of town where she had arranged with a family to keep a cow for her. She had nurtured the animal since it was a calf and named her Jina (pronounced Yeena). Jina provided milk for Philomene and her family.

"Because my mother spoke perfect Russian, she became an interpreter for the German army. She was given a nice house next to the Black Sea in the area where the higher officers lived with their families."

So Philomene and her daughter moved from the Deutsche Haus to a villa where they could see the Black Sea from their porch. Philomene had reclaimed her family name—Keller—and her daughter now had a new surname. Philomena made friends quickly among the children of other military workers who lived in apartments within the compound.

Philomena never knew the significance of her mother's role with the German army. Only as an adult did she begin to piece together hints of the world her mother entered when she went to work each day—hints like the little gold box.

"I was playing with my friends where my mother worked. The iron gate of the compound was open. A big truck rolled in and dumped a mountain of clothes and some shoes on the ground. My mother had told me not to take any clothes brought in by a truck. I obeyed, even when the driver said, 'Help yourselves.'*

"The clothes disappeared quickly. My girlfriend urged me to try on a pair of shoes with high heels the way she did. I remember trying to walk in the shoes. They hurt my feet and I took them off. I would not have been allowed to keep them anyway.

"But there on the ground next to the clothes and shoes was a glistening object, not a piece of clothing, but a tiny gold box. I picked it up. It opened like a book. It was a little book with a cover of gold metal. Inside were tiny pages of very thin parchment with tiny, tiny foreign lettering on them. I was fascinated. It fitted perfectly into my small hand when I closed it. I thought it was beautiful and took it home, as we were invited to do. My mother explained to me that it was sacred and I should honor it. I am sure she recognized that it was a miniature Torah, but she told me it was like a Bible and should be respected. She allowed me to keep it as something secret.

"My mother must have known where those clothes came from, but we never talked about it. I can only imagine what she knew. It still presses on my heart when I think of it."

Philomena's "German people's school" identification card (with her nickname "Mina") issued after the Germans occupied Odessa and she took her mother's family name. Volksdeutsche was the name given to people of German language and culture living outside the borders of Germany, having migrated eastward, especially in previous centuries.

Part II

FLIGHT

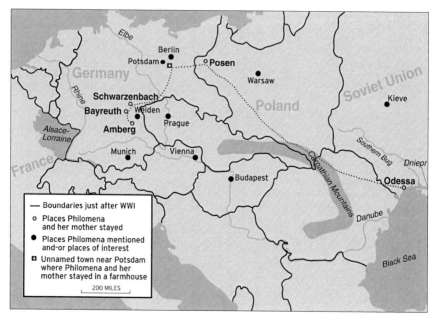

German refugees traveled from Odessa across the Carpathian Mountains into Poland and eventually to Germany. (*Bangor Daily News* map)

3
The Train Ride

Boxcars of refugees

The success of the German invasion of the Soviet Union rose and fell between 1941 and 1944. The Red Army gradually reclaimed territories occupied by Germany—Kharkov, Kiev, Leningrad, bridgeheads on the Dnieper River—until by March 1944 only two places remained under German occupation: the Crimea and Odessa.

One day Philomene came home from work early. The Soviet army was advancing toward Odessa. German civilians were to be evacuated. Philomene's position with the German military entitled her and her family to passage out of Odessa in one of two freight cars for civilians attached to a train carrying wounded German soldiers. They would have to be ready by 3 p.m. the next day.

"We were to gather in a wooded area where the train would be hidden under the trees to conceal it from the low-flying Russian airplanes policing the vicinity. The train would leave at sunset and travel under the cloak of darkness.

"My mother raced to the Deutsche Haus to tell her sister Julia. Then she took a streetcar out to the farm to say good-bye to Jina. She loved that cow and left it tearfully in the care of the friends who had kept it for her, bringing back some milk for our journey."

Meanwhile, Julia instructed her son, Alfred, to go to the market and buy three live geese. He remembered years later that he had to kill them himself, which he had never done before. His mother then preserved the meat in jars, to be shared among family members during their journey, one small piece at a time.

When Philomene returned from the country, Julia was ready with the children and their 75-year-old aunt. The family squeezed into a streetcar packed with anxious civilians. They arrived at the

31

designated spot in the woods. A crowd was assembling and the train was waiting. The doors to the boxcars slid open and people began to climb in. Philomena was the last to board.

"As I approached the train, I turned back and stopped, spellbound by the beauty of the golden rays of the sun. I sensed the gravity of what we were doing and thought to myself, 'I want to remember that sunset for the rest of my life.' And I have, to this day. When I turned around, everyone was on the train. I was all alone. I heard my name and grabbed the hand that pulled me into the boxcar."

The big doors rolled shut and Philomena Keller became part of a massive German retreat from the advancing Russians. With the beauty of a sunset—her last view of Odessa—etched in her memory, 9-year-old Philomena began a ride through the snow-covered Carpathian Mountains in a car designed to transport animals.

She was privileged to be associated with the German military, thanks to her mother's position as an interpreter. Later they learned that Germans who remained in Odessa were either shot or sent to Siberia. Philomena, her family and others crowded into the two boxcars were among the last German civilians to leave.

The train ride would end in German-occupied Poland where the refugees would be given German citizenship. But Philomena was unaware of the destination or the significance of the trip.

She felt safe with her mother and relatives, huddled on the floor of the cold freight car with their few belongings, the light from small rectangular windows near the ceiling indicating when night turned to day. They shared the meat and canned food they had brought from their pantries, but it was not enough for the entire trip. Occasionally, they would receive leftovers from the cars carrying the wounded soldiers.

"We were on the train a couple of weeks. It was very cold. Snow stays on the ground all year in the Carpathian Mountains. After a while there was nothing to eat. When the train passed through Hungary, people in the villages were waiting for it. They

Philomena before she was evacuated from Odessa with her family in 1944.

Philomene on the porch of the villa provided for her and her daughter by the German army within the confines of the military installation on the outskirts of Odessa, where she worked as an interpreter after the occupation in June 1941.

had heard that a refugee train was coming. The train slowed down in the villages, but did not stop. We opened the freight-car doors and saw villagers standing on the platform with bags full of bread. They threw the loaves through the open doors of the boxcar for the refugees to catch."

Twice a day the train would stop to take on water for the steam locomotives from hidden wells in remote areas. During these stops, the refugees were allowed to get out of the boxcars to stretch their legs, breathe fresh air and relieve themselves. The medical cars were fully equipped for the soldiers, but there were no facilities in the boxcars. Passengers would spread out in the uninhabited wooded areas away from the tracks. The train whistle blew three times to call them back. The last whistle meant the train was ready to move. After one of these stops, Philomena could not find her mother when the doors to the boxcar had closed.

"Where is my mother?" she asked.

"Oh, she is probably in one of the other cars talking to the wounded soldiers," her relatives responded.

But Philomena sensed their restlessness. They looked concerned.

Years later, long after Philomena had moved to the United States, her cousin Viktoria told her exactly what had happened. No one had wanted her to know that after that fateful rest stop, her mother was missing.

Apparently, Philomene's modesty had led her too far from the track to return to the train in time. She was alone in a vast land of snow when she heard the whistle. She started to run. She climbed up the snowy embankment to the tracks, but she had not reached the train when it started to move.

A man in the rear car, perhaps a medical assistant, saw her and shouted encouragement. Then more and more people saw her. They yelled and cheered as she ran to keep up. The snow slowed her down. The man stepped out onto the bottom step of the stairs, grasping the handrail with one hand and reaching for Philomene's outstretched hand with the other.

"Viktoria still gets emotional when she tells the story," Philomena says, recalling her cousin's words: "That picture is absolutely indescribable—your mother running through the snow and how everyone was cheering her on and how that man risked his life to save her when he reached out his hand for her to grab. It was a miracle that she had the strength to catch up to the train and grasp the hand that drew her to safety."

"I had no idea," said Philomena. "When we were reunited in the boxcar it was as though nothing had happened. No one wanted me to know. They did not want me to worry."

The long train ride ended in Posen, Poland, where the refugees were hustled off the train onto the station platform. "I remember coming out of the train hardly believing we had arrived. My mother said, 'Finally, we have arrived.' Immediately we were ushered into a room where we received our German citizenship papers. It was all very secretive and quickly done, so no one else would intrude and the processing would be legitimate. I looked at the date on my paper: June 1, 1944. In five days I would be 10 years of age."

With the land of her birth behind her, Philomena now belonged to the country of her mother's ancestors, a nation facing defeat in a war begun when she was 5 with the invasion of Poland, where she now stood. The Germans had gotten her out of Odessa, but she and her family were not yet safe from the Russians. She had just begun her flight to freedom, most of which would be on foot.

The photo on Philomene's German passport, issued upon arrival in Posen, Poland, after she was evacuated from Odessa.

4
German-Occupied Poland

The last time we saw Josef

Josef Hartmann in the German army uniform he was so proud to wear that it cost him his life (1945).

"We were taken to a little town called Netzen, about 15 kilometers from Posen," Philomena recalled. "We were given a house that had been vacated by its owners. It was a nice little house beside a road going through a small village. We stayed there for about nine months. My mother, with her good education, was trained to run the post office there and to operate the telephone switchboard. She taught me to connect phone calls, often from soldiers calling home from their stations."

Philomena's Aunt Julia and her family lived diagonally across the road on a farm. Josef, the oldest son, had volunteered to join the German army. Viktoria, Angelika and Alfred were old enough to do farm work. Johannes and Philomena were too young to work. When the school year began, they took a bus every day to attend school in Schlehen, about 10 kilometers away. Different ages of students were grouped together in one classroom.

"All of a sudden I could speak German. It was easy to learn among my new German-speaking friends. I still remember the day I missed the bus home. It was winter. The parents of one of my school friends wanted me to stay with them that night, but I insisted on walking home. Snow began to fall and the wind blew. I was wearing a skirt and sweater, stockings and shoes, no boots. The snow was deep by the time I reached home. My shoes and stockings were soaked. I could not feel my toes. As always, my mother displayed no alarm or anxiety, just pleasure that I was home safe. I wondered what would have happened if I had died and they didn't find me until spring. Still today I can see myself pushing against the wind-driven snow."

When spring arrived, word spread among the refugees that the Soviet army was beginning to encircle the area and they should prepare to leave. Josef was visiting his family on leave and called his military unit for instructions on how to rejoin his

Julia Hartmann with her children Angelika, Johannes, Josef (in uniform), Viktoria and Alfred (Summer 1943).

company. He was told he had been cut off from his unit and was given permission to flee with his family.

"Word got around that we were to leave in the morning. Because we were the youngest, Johannes, who was 9, and I, age 10, would ride in a wagon with the 75-year-old Aunt Julia, who was not well. Everyone else would walk."

Josef and his brother Alfred searched for a vehicle to pull the wagon. They found an old abandoned tractor in a field on the farm where they were staying and resolved to get it running. Its owners doubted it was possible.

"They worked all night with flashlights. Finally they got the tractor running. They attached it to a wagon full of straw for Johannes and me and our aunt."

The next morning, Josef insisted on wearing his army uniform. His mother protested, warning him she thought it would be dangerous. But he wanted to make a political statement and joined the mass of walking refugees as a member of the German military.

"The road was packed with people anxious to get away from the approaching Russians. The straw made a nice cushion in the wagon for my cousin, Johannes, our aunt and me. We felt fortunate to have padded transportation, but soon we, too, had to walk. When the tractor ran out of gas, we had to leave it behind.

"All of a sudden there was a commotion. A Volkswagen came toward us and stopped on the roadside. A German officer covered with medals stepped out of the car. He pointed to Josef. Josef stood at attention. The officer demanded his ID. A few words were exchanged and the door of the Volkswagen was opened. Josef got in, the vehicle took off and we never saw Josef again.

"Can you imagine? His mother was there, his aunt was crying. There was no way to communicate with the official who had told him by phone to stay with his family. The officer didn't believe he had tried to rejoin his company. We learned much later that Josef had been shot as a deserter."

5

Potsdam

Separation and reunion

Philomena, her mother, her aunts and cousins were homeless, walking with other German refugees toward an uncertain destination—west. Only military vehicles were allowed fuel. Everyone else walked. They were moving toward Berlin. Julia and her sister Philomene had an understanding that if they got separated they would go toward Berlin and contact the Red Cross to try to find each other.

"At one point, word spread among the refugees that a westbound train was coming in our direction. The station platform was jammed. Everyone wanted to be on that train. Aunt Julia, her four children and our older aunt squeezed into one of the cars. The train started to move. People were clinging to the doors and windows."

After the train pulled away, Philomena and her mother were left with many others standing on the platform. They waited for the next train, but it never came. They learned it had been bombed by Russian airplanes.

So the stranded refugees continued to walk. When it got dark, Philomena and her mother stopped in a village and slept curled up together under a tree. The next day, they found the town office where the Burgermeister (chief town official) directed them to a family who had offered space for refugees to stay for a temporary rest.

German towns and villages were ready for the refugees from the Soviet Union. Residents who had space to offer in homes, barns and vacant buildings registered in the town office. When refugees entered a village or town, they looked for the Burgermeister who would help them find shelter with the families who had registered. They also received coupons to redeem for food.

Philomena speaks fondly of the young mother who welcomed them to her small farmhouse about 20 kilometers from Potsdam, where she was living with her infant daughter and her mother while her husband was off at war. Philomena and her mother had been there for some time with no idea where Julia and her family were, when a coincidence brought the two families back together.

"I was walking to visit a school friend one afternoon and saw a girl getting off a bicycle beside the highway. She looked just like my cousin Viktoria. I called to her. She looked up and recognized me immediately. We rushed into each other's arms. It was unbelievable, a surreal moment!"

Philomena's older cousin, Viktoria, had set out on a borrowed bicycle to look for her relatives. She was cycling from village to village asking the Burgermeister in each town if anyone named Keller had requested a place to stay. She had been riding most of the day when Philomena spotted her.

"I took Viktoria to the farmhouse where we were staying to see my mother and meet the lady of the house. Viktoria and her family had been taken in by an opera singer who lived in a lovely apartment in a tall ornate building in Potsdam. She would fill the place with music when she practiced, sometimes even when they were trying to sleep. We took the train to visit Aunt Julia and our cousins in Potsdam several times before we had to flee again."

But soon it was time to leave. The Soviet army was moving closer to Potsdam. "We kids were told to take refuge in any building if we heard planes when we were playing outside. Russian aircraft would fly low and shoot people in the streets, even children. The sirens would go off and people would run from the streets into any house or shelter whenever planes were spotted. We never knew what the Russians would be doing next. We depended on hearsay and spies for the news.

"To get to church on Sunday we would walk approximately 12 kilometers on a path through the woods. Then suddenly word spread that Russians had parachuted into the area around the church. Typically, paratroopers would stay until the army arrived to occupy an area. When my mother heard that paratroopers had landed and tanks were moving in, she said we had to leave immediately.

"People in town began to pull together knapsacks and whatever they could get to carry supplies. My mother had been carrying documents and treasured family photographs, including pictures of ancestors, up to this point. We had said our goodbyes and were heading out when she decided to leave the photographs with our host family, with the understanding that she would return some day to get them. As we were departing for a second time, the farm wife came running after us with her baby's stroller, insisting we use it to carry some of our things. She had just baked bread and gave us a loaf for our trip. That stroller was such a blessing. People who had taken more than they could carry had to leave their belongings beside the road."

Philomena and her mother planned to take a train to Potsdam where they would meet Julia and her family. From there they would travel together on the train coming from Berlin bound for Allied-occupied Munich. But they had a contingency plan, in case they became separated again.

"A friend of Angelika in Potsdam had told her about a place in Bavaria called Barbaraberg, near the village of Weiden. She wrote the name of the town on a piece of paper for Angelika to take with her. My mother and Aunt Julia agreed that we would meet in Barbaraberg, if we became separated."

The plan was well-conceived. The two families were separated before their journey even began. The train Philomena and her mother were to take to Potsdam never came. It was destroyed by Russian dive-bombers.

"We walked away on foot. It was springtime. The apple and cherry trees were in full bloom. They looked beautiful. I thought, 'This is how I will remember the time we left, by the blossoming trees.'"

Part III

THE LONG WALK

6

To the Elbe River

"A moving carpet of people"

Philomena and her mother were alone. They had no idea where Julia and her family were. They just kept walking. They learned they would be safe if they could cross the Elbe River. They had no maps. They just kept asking people for the way to the river. Roadsides were littered with things people had cast aside to lighten their loads and with civilian cars and trucks abandoned when their tanks ran dry.

Scorched Earth

As the German army retreated, it left a trail of destruction to hinder the advance of the Russians. Hitler ordered that timed explosives be set to wipe out bridges and rip up railroad tracks behind his army as it moved west. This "scorched earth" policy also impeded Philomena and her mother. They had just left the friendly family that had given them shelter near Potsdam when they were thrown to the ground by the power of an explosion.

"To reach the highway we had to cross an overpass. We crossed the bridge and were walking toward the highway. We were no more than 100 or 250 feet beyond the bridge when it exploded—a timed explosive set by the Germans to slow down the Russians. My mother threw herself on top of me and debris covered our bodies. If we had been a few minutes later the bridge would have been gone, or we might have been on it.

"People were moving shoulder to shoulder along the highway to get out of the village. They ran into the woods when the bridge exploded, but gradually returned to the highway. My mother said, 'Let's get away from the crowd,' and led me into a wooded area to avoid low-flying airplanes attacking those who were fleeing. We walked on a footpath beside the highway just deep enough into the trees that we could see the highway but not be exposed. Sure enough, dive-bombers appeared after a while, killing and wounding many people. So we stayed away from the masses.

"We walked until dark and slept outside under the trees. We found mushrooms to eat, brooks for water and shadow for rest. We wanted to get as far away from the Russians as we could. I remember it was nice and warm and there were stars in the sky. We awoke early the next day and started walking again. Sometimes people would come out of their houses and give us food, especially older people and mothers with children.

"In one small village we came to a river. People told us all the bridges over that river had been demolished. However, as we walked, we saw one bridge with the rails and ties still intact. 'We *must* cross this bridge,' my mother said. She left the stroller behind and tied necessary items onto her back. She said, 'Stay behind me, watch what I do, do what I do.' On our hands and knees we crawled across the ties, one hand and one foot at a time, while the river roared beneath us. The rails were a good three feet apart. At one point there were only a couple of ties to crawl on, but we could not turn back. My mother kept saying, 'Don't look down, just look ahead.' We held on for our lives and made it across. When we got to the other side my mother sat down on the ground and pulled me to her, holding me tight and shedding tears of gratitude. She praised me for being a brave girl. This was the first and last time I saw my mother cry. She never let me see her fears."

Shelter

"We walked many days, sometimes given food and shelter by kind locals. When we sat down to rest, my mother would entertain me by drawing a map or doing arithmetic with a branch in the sand. She made things fun. She was a teacher by profession, and she would show me where the oceans were, where we were, where we were going. She told me about America, where buildings were so tall they swayed at the top."

Periodically word would spread among the refugees, often through townspeople, that the Russians had been pushed back and they could stay longer in their temporary homes. Philomena remembers one such stay about 17 kilometers from the Elbe River.

"I can still see the house with a big arch leading into a brick yard and stables. They had horses with colts and cows with calves. I think we stayed there about 10 days." Inevitably, the relative calm would be shattered by word the Russians were advancing. "One had to be prepared every minute to get up and go.

"We were walking in the same direction as the German army. We were still hopeful that they would reclaim that part of Germany. We had heard the Germans were winning this area back, but in fact they were being surrounded and pressed into a 'kettle.' We were in one of the places where the German army was mounting its last defense."

Surrender

"We got word that the Germans were ready to surrender. The Elbe River divided the territory being occupied by the Russians from the land occupied by the [Western] Allies. It was important for the Germans to cross the river as quickly as possible. Word got around that the Americans were humane. So that's where everyone was aiming to go—toward the Americans. Crowds of desperate Germans—civilians and soldiers—moved toward the river

"We saw young German soldiers—just boys, 16, 17, 18 years of age. Some were badly wounded, with missing limbs and bleeding arms, legs and faces. One soldier said he had been in a trench when a grenade exploded. Another, without a leg, walked on crutches. They all wanted to cross the river before the Russians arrived. People stepped aside when military vehicles moved through the crowd.

"One open military vehicle stopped in the midst of the moving crowd next to my mother and me. An officer decorated with medals was sitting behind the driver. Another officer sat next to the driver. '*Steigen Sie ein*'('Step in'), said the officer in back. 'We'll give you a ride,' and he helped us into the vehicle. He asked my mother where we were from and pointed to me. He said he had children my age and he didn't know if they were alive. 'They don't know where I am,' he said. He offered me candy and rations—food they should have eaten—and they gave us a ride to the Elbe River. Without that ride, we certainly would have been left in the hands of the Russians who were coming behind us. We would not have made it to the river before dark.

"The river banks were overflowing with people. We saw a boat on our side of the river. We heard that it was ferrying Germans across to the American side. Finally, we would be safe. But then the decision was made that only surrendering German soldiers would be allowed to cross the river. The single ferry was no longer allowed to transport civilians.

"The shore became a moving carpet of people, begging and crying. There were so many people you couldn't even see the ground. My mother motioned: 'Follow me, let's get away from the crowd.' So we walked away from the ferry.

"My mother and I came to a cove by the river. We could see through an opening in the bushes that there was a barge loaded with coal hidden in the cove. A German officer and his company of 18 men were throwing coal off the barge so they could load it with men to cross to the American side. They planned to take half the men across and then come back for the others. My mother asked to go with them. The captain looked at us and said, 'If you help us get the coal off, you can come with us.' There were no shovels, so we worked with our bare hands.

"A young mother in tears with an infant in her arms and a

toddler by her side begged to come along. She too started to help remove the coal. Other soldiers began to arrive, including wounded soldiers needing help. The German officer shed tears when he saw how many people needed to get across the river. The boat would soon be overloaded. It would have to make several trips while the Russians were pushing toward the river. My mother was moved that the officer left half of his men behind to make room for us and the other civilians."

It was late in the afternoon when the barge was light enough to move away from the shore carrying Philomena, her mother, the woman with the two children, other civilians, wounded soldiers and the officer with half of the men from his company. It started to rain halfway across the river and was still raining when they arrived. At the American side, civilians were separated from the German soldiers who were officially received as prisoners of war. The German commanding officer stepped forward: "We are here to surrender," he said to the American officer.

"The humility of surrendering really touched my mother. As prisoners of war the soldiers had to turn over their weapons, jewelry, tools and maps, but the Russians would have been worse, they would have killed them. They were blessed to be surrendering to the Americans, who were very humane. My mother later confessed that tears came to her eyes when she saw the German soldiers, now prisoners, taking off their wedding bands. All pieces of jewelry were considered weapons.

"The Americans asked the civilians to stay together in a separate spot while the soldiers surrendered. The American and German officers spoke to each other through an interpreter. It was still raining, and it was getting dark.

"The wet grass was as high as my shoulders, but I could see everything. The gravity of this experience only came to me much later when I heard my mother telling this story to others.

"The German officer begged for permission to return for the rest of his men so they could surrender as a company. The request was granted. Now that's humanity! Who but Americans would have allowed that? Russians would not have allowed it."

Nonetheless, the American officers did not allow the German civilians to remain on the American side. Philomena, her mother and the other civilians were turned away from the American shore. They had to return to the coal boat with the German officer to be ferried back to the side of the river soon to be occupied by the Russians.

"Everybody broke down crying when they learned they had to return, but the Americans obeyed their orders: no civilians. We walked back to the boat in the rain, the tall, wet grass sweeping my shoulders. We boarded in the dark of the night and sat down on the wet coal."

The Elbe is known for sandbars that can appear unexpectedly and damage a boat. Halfway across the river, the barge got stranded—good fortune for the civilians who were being returned, but the German officer was beside himself with concern for the troops who were hidden in the cove waiting to be rescued.

"Again, we threw out more coal with our bare hands to make the boat lighter, but nothing we did was helping. In the middle of the night, we heard shots—the Russians announcing their arrival on the eastern shore of the river. The Americans responded with shots from the opposite shore. Then the Russian soldiers returned to the village we had just left.

"The German officer shed tears for fear his men would fall into the hands of the Russians. He had risked the safety of his soldiers to make room for civilians, some with children. The woman with the two children used her camisole to make a white flag of neutrality to help protect our boat from a possible attack.

"At sunrise, we could see the banks of the American side clearly. The ferry was gone. No Russians were in sight. But we were stuck in the middle of the river. Then we saw a fisherman in a small canoe-sized boat. It was Sunday and he wanted to do some fishing before church. The German officer asked him to take us across to the American side of the river. The fisherman said his boat was too small, but he promised to return with a larger one. We did not believe we would see him again, but he did return in a larger boat with a motor. He took the civilians first; then he went back for the German soldiers who were waiting in the cove on the Russian side of the river.

"Once again, we got out of the boat into the tall, wet grass. American jeeps drove back and forth patrolling the shore. The American soldiers saw us, but this time they looked the other way. They allowed us to continue our journey to freedom."

7
American-Occupied Germany

Another unlikely reunion

For Philomena and her mother, crossing the Elbe River into the American-occupied zone of Germany meant safety. And they were there, thanks to the compassion of American soldiers who let them scramble onto the shore after a rainy night of uncertainty on the river. But their relief was interrupted by a loudspeaker.

"There was an announcement that civilians who crossed during the night should register. They might have been asking us to register for food rations, but my mother was not about to take the chance of being returned to the Russian side of the river. We moved away as quickly as we could."

Their destination was Barbaraberg where they had agreed to meet Philomena's Aunt Julia, her cousins and older aunt. They knew only that it was near Weiden. And so Philomena and her mother began to walk. The Burgermeister in each village helped them find lodging for the night. Sometimes they slept on straw or hay in barns with the animals.

"I remember sleeping in a stable with horses and goats. Resting on the soft hay surrounded by peaceful animals I asked my mother, 'Is this how Jesus slept?'"

One morning after a night in a barn Philomena awoke at sunrise to the sound of kittens mewing. "I got up without waking my mother and followed the sound to a little nest of kittens with their eyes still closed. The mother cat was washing them. She came to me and rubbed against me, and then went back to her kittens. They were so cute. They really brightened up the world for me. I picked one up and took it to show my mother. In her usual calm way she suggested I put it back so its mother would not worry.

"I have learned one big lesson from that period of time: Children behave as their parents do. If parents panic, so will their children. My mother never left me guessing. She explained the situations tailored for a child. She was calm so I didn't experience fear. Even now I seldom panic.

"We weren't running away anymore. We walked and walked. When our shoes wore out, we walked on our bare feet. The tar road burned our feet and the sun scorched our skin. One morning we awoke and my mother was so badly burned we had to stop."

They found the Burgermeister in the nearest village. All the town's doctors had been drawn into the war and there was no hospital. Sick and injured people were spread out on the floor of a school on straw mats. They found a place for Philomena's mother in this makeshift hospital and gave her daughter a mat by her side.

"We must have been there 10 days. She was covered with severe burns. I picked a bouquet of field flowers for her and we used a drinking glass for a vase. I was so happy to bring her some cheer. So was she.

"When we were finally able to continue, I remember walking on a sidewalk early one morning with houses on the left and a park on the right. There in the road was a small coin purse. I asked if I could pick it up. My mother said OK, maybe we can find out who owns it. There was no name or other identification inside the purse. It contained a few coins and two rings made out of coins, a wedding ring and a ring with a flat surface that could be engraved—a signet ring.

"At that time people didn't have much jewelry. They made rings from coins. I had always wanted a signet ring and the one in the purse fit me perfectly. The wedding band fit my mother. I begged to keep the rings so we could wear them. My mother wanted to find the owner of the purse, but no one was around. I wanted to keep the purse. It was as if God had dropped it down to give us a little happiness."

Philomena wore her ring, but her mother would use the other ring to express gratitude. Toward the end of that day they were walking with other refugees through a village where townspeople were waiting on the sidewalks to offer them places to stay overnight. Philomena and her mother were welcomed into a family that made them feel like royalty. The hostess' parents and great-grandparents lived there, but her husband and son were in the war. No one knew where they were.

"It was unbelievable. They had a beautiful room prepared with two beds, clean sheets, feather down mattresses and running water. We were able to take a bath. It was like being in heaven. Then they invited us to eat with them. They pushed tables together to make a long table for dinner, covered it with a beautiful cloth and set out beautiful dishes, silver tableware and linens. They put us at the head of the table and served a wonderful meal fit for royalty. It was a beautiful evening for all of us.

"They liked to bring in refugees. They showed us the husband's stamp collections and attributed their good fortune during the war to their faithful attendance at church. They traveled 15 kilometers in a carriage to church every Sunday and holiday, rain or shine. This house was full of love.

"Sleeping on those soft pillows and the feather bed in that house I had a dream. I told my mother that I dreamed I saw a sign and it pointed to Barbaraberg. My mother paid attention to my dreams.

"When we left the next morning after a nice breakfast, the people had tears in their eyes. I was wearing my ring, but I noticed as we walked that my mother was not wearing hers. 'Why aren't you wearing your ring?' I asked. My mother changed the subject. Eventually she told me she had given it to the woman at the house whose husband was in the war. She wanted to give her something in return for her kindness— the nice place to stay and the beautiful dinner.

"We saw only one vehicle. As we walked along the highway

on the sidewalk, a truck full of gravel stopped in the road. The driver asked where we were headed. 'Barbaraberg,' we said.

'Where's that?' he asked.

'Near Weiden,' we said.

'*Steigen Sie ein*' (Hop in), he said."

The man in the passenger seat jumped out and said he would ride atop the gravel to make room for them next to the driver. Philomene protested, but he insisted. They rode all the way to Weiden, saving hours of walking. As they got out of the truck, the workmen tried to guide them toward their destination, even though they had not heard of Barbaraberg.

"We started to inquire where there might be a Barbaraberg. Someone said it was probably in the area of Schwarzenbach.

'How far is that to walk?'

'Well, if you walk through the woods you might get there by day's end.'

"So we found the pathway through the woods and started walking. We came to an intersection. A post with signs for several unfamiliar places lay on the ground.

"My mother remembered my dream about seeing the sign to Barbaraberg. 'Which way should we go?' she asked. She often let me decide things like that and I chose the path we would take. We came to a little lake in the forest. There was one house by that lake where, we learned later, a forest ranger lived with his family. It was a beautiful red-brick building and we thought perhaps we could stop for the night. We knocked several times, but there was no answer so we continued walking.

"We came out of the woods into an opening and a rise in the road. As we walked up the hill we could see the steeple of a church and the roofs of houses. My mother was in a hurry because it was getting late and she wanted to find the town office before dark to sign up for the night.

"We came to a level spot in the road with a row of trees and a ditch on the left side and houses on the right. Unfolding before us was a village called Schwarzenbach. I had been carrying a walking stick that I carved with a folding knife along the way. At that spot, I tossed the stick into the ditch on our left. My mother asked why I did that and I said I just felt like leaving it there.

'But you have carved such nice things on it,' she said.

'I will carve another stick,' I said cheerfully.

"As we approached the center of the village, church bells began to ring. It was the month of May when prayer services in honor of the Virgin Mary were held every evening at 6 p.m. We had attended these services in other villages and would have attended in this village if we had arrived earlier."

The service was over and people were filing out of the church. Philomena stopped to watch.

"Come, we must find a place to stay," her mother urged. But Philomena kept looking back as they passed the church. Suddenly she called out.

"Tante Julia! Angelika! Johannes!" And she ran off yelling.

"My mother thought, 'Oh, she'll be coming back disappointed.'"

But when Philomene looked back, her daughter was wrapped in the arms of the aunt and cousins they had not seen since they had parted in Potsdam.

"They came over to my mother and it was quite a reunion. Alfred and Viktoria weren't with them because they were working for a farmer nearby and had to feed and prepare the animals for the night. They could not go to church in the evening because they had to get up very early in the morning to milk the cows. We didn't see them until the next day.

"While the others were shedding tears of joy, my cousin Johannes, who is near my age, and I started running around chasing each other. I told him that I had just thrown away a stick I had been carving, and we ran off to find the stick."

The two families headed for the house where Aunt Julia, her daughter Angelika and son Johannes were living. The house was directly opposite the ditch where Philomena had thrown away her stick. "My mother couldn't believe it. I kept that stick for quite some time."

Aunt Julia, her children and the elderly aunt had caught the last train out of Berlin before the city fell to the Russians. During the night, their train bound for Munich was attacked by Russian planes. It stopped near a wooded area so the passengers could jump out and hide. People scattered into the woods where they spent the night. They had no idea where they were, but started walking the next morning.

Julia's family eventually reached Weiden, where they stayed two weeks while officials found places for them to live. At last they were assigned to jobs that suited their skills in the village of Schwarzenbach.

"There were no men older than 16 in the village. They all had been drafted. Women did everything. Everyone lived off the farms, and the fields needed to be worked. They welcomed people who could help them."

Julia, Angelika and Johannes lived in a house that served as a day care center for farmers' children. Angelika, who was trained as a child educator, had a job caring for local children during the day while their mothers were working in the fields. Julia prepared meals for the children. Alfred and Viktoria lived in a farmhouse where they cared for the animals used in the fields. They arose early in the morning to feed and water the animals and clean the barns, chores that were repeated in the evening.

And what about Barbaraberg, the place where they were to rendezvous? They discovered it was not even a town. It was just a hill serving as pasture for the animals of local farmers.

How could it be that both families would find their way to the tiny village of Schwarzenbach by such different routes? It seemed like more than coincidence.

Part IV

FREEDOM

8

Bavaria

Getting to know the Americans

Philomena (center) was one of seven girls who were the first girls to pass the test qualifying them for enrollment in gymnasium in Bayreuth after the war.

Philomena and her mother spent the summer of 1945 with her Aunt Julia and her cousins in Schwarzenbach. During that time Philomena's older cousins learned about housing for refugees. Twenty kilometers away, in Bayreuth, Hitler had ordered the construction of emergency homes called "Behelfsheime" [make-do homes]. Space was available on a first-come, first-served basis. Several times, Alfred, Angelika and Philomene got up at 4 a.m. and walked to Bayreuth along the railroad tracks, returning to Schwarzenbach on the same day. Finally they were able to reserve space in a Behelfsheim, where Philomena and her mother moved in the fall.

Above: Philomena sits in the second row on the left (wearing a white collar) among the girls admitted to gymnasium in a 1940s class photo in Bayreuth.

Left: Philomena's mother doing farm work in Bayreuth, Germany, (c. 1945).

Below: Philomena demonstrates how to frame a photograph on a photo tour for military personnel and their dependents from the U.S. Army base in Amberg, Germany, (c. 1949).

"It was a simple double structure with a shed roof and two unfurnished apartments containing only a woodstove and a few built-in cabinets. We entered through a common door into a small foyer with an apartment on either side. An apartment consisted of a kitchen and a smaller room containing a bed made out of boards. It was meager, but we felt lucky. Other families had lost their homes and everything in them to the merciless bombings of the war."

Bayreuth

"Bayreuth was heaped with the rubble of war. We had to climb over mountains of debris to get from place to place. The streets and sidewalks were full of stones, pieces of fallen buildings and dust. In the remains of bombed-out houses we could see furnishings—desks, beds, chairs—still standing in rooms with fragments of walls."

Every morning 10-year-old Philomena spent several hours in a long line, container in hand, waiting for her daily ration of two cups of milk. She would get up before dawn to get in line by 4 a.m.

"Often rations of food and milk ran out before everyone was served, so people arrived before dawn and stood for hours in the dark. If adults were fortunate enough to have jobs, they would send their children to stand in line for the day's rations."

One day, as Philomena walked home with her milk, she was surprised to see her mother weeding a field behind a tall wire fence enclosing a large piece of land cultivated with rows of vegetables. Philomena called and waved, but her mother gestured that she should hurry along and not linger by the fence that separated them.

"I wondered why she did not greet me happily. She explained to me later that she was fortunate to have a job, even a menial one. She was very conscientious and would not want her supervisors to think she would allow a distraction. Now that I am a mother,

American soldiers
entertain German
children with
holiday gifts.

I can imagine how difficult it must have been for her to see me on the other side of that fence and not be able to respond to me as she would have liked to. She found herself in a situation where her hands were tied.

"In order to have flour we gathered the wheat berries that were left in the fields after the harvest and took them to a mill to be ground. We tied cloths around our waists to collect the grains. It was painful to walk on the cut-off wheat with our bare feet, but we needed flour. To avoid the pain of walking, we were taught to flatten the cut stalks by sliding our feet into the spaces between the rows."

One sunny day Philomena was startled when a man in his 40s, carrying his shirt and wearing no shoes, approached her and her friends where they were playing near the Behelfsheim.

"He asked for Ida, but we didn't recognize him. It was my mother's cousin, Leo, Ida's husband. We called him Uncle Leo. He had escaped from a prison and walked from the Russian-occupied sector of Germany. He had worked in the kitchen of the prison where he learned that too much vinegar would make the heart pump faster. He drank enough vinegar to increase his heart rate to a level that qualified him for release as an ill person.

(The Russians released prisoners who were ill.) He learned from the Red Cross where his family was living and found us at the Behelfsheim settlement in Bayreuth."

The Americans

"Not long after my mother and I had settled in the city of Bayreuth, which was occupied by the American army, we were walking near the edge of town when we came upon a crowd of people at a railroad crossing. The gate was down. Someone shouted, 'There it is. The train is coming!' It was a train of American soldiers, leaning out the windows and hanging onto the doors, throwing showers of candies for the children in the crowd. We were still collecting the tightly wrapped candies after the train had passed when my mother gently tapped me on the shoulder, looked lovingly into my eyes and suggested I be grateful for what I had already and leave the rest of the sweets for those who needed them more than I did."

On holidays soldiers from the U.S. Army base in Bayreuth introduced German children to American traditions and games that were new and fun for them.

"They would get the children together for holiday games they had played at home. They organized Easter egg hunts and three-legged races—games we had never heard of in Germany—and gave candies for prizes. At these times they were not soldiers, they were young men away from home. They were doing nice things for the children, and I was one of those children. We were fortunate to be in the part of Germany occupied by the Americans. We looked up to them. They were kind and understanding. I often wondered how they felt being so far away from their homes and families."

Yet even in western Germany, Philomena and her family were not safe. The Russians ordered Germans who had fled from Russia to be returned, and began rounding them up to be transported to Russia by train. Philomena's Aunt Maria, who had been shot in the hip by the Russians when she was pregnant, was put on a train with her family and returned to Russia. Much later, Viktoria arranged for them to leave Russia and to settle in West Germany where they lived a good life.

Fortunately, Philomena and her relatives had obtained documents identifying them as being from Alsace-Lorraine—the home of their ancestors between France and Germany from which Germans in the colonies around Odessa had come in the 1800s.

"My mother, her oldest sister and all of us children were now from Alsace, not Russia."

Gymnasium

Gradually schools that had served as hospitals during the war were reopened as schools and Philomena entered at the sixth-grade level. At the end of sixth grade, she was one of the first girls allowed to take the exam for admission to the "gymnasium," the German school that prepares students for professions, such as law, medicine and the priesthood, requiring higher education and a foundation in Latin, Greek and English. She and six other girls passed the exam and went on to the Humanistisches Gymnasium.

"At that time only men were expected to pursue higher education and professions while women stayed at home to raise the children and tend the house. Things are different now."

After Philomena completed her education in Bayreuth, she learned about a vacancy in the library of the U.S. Army base where her mother worked. The librarian encouraged her to apply. But even though she was fluent in Russian and German and had studied English, along with Greek and Latin, Philomena did not trust herself to speak English well enough for such a position. "In Germany everything had to be perfect."

The librarian said, "Don't worry. I will prepare you for the interview." She knew what Philomena would be asked, and

U.S. Army Master Sergeant John A. Baker
of Fort Kent in Amberg, Germany (1950s).

Philomena in the photo lab of the U.S. Army
base in Amberg, Germany, where she served
military personnel and their dependents.

Self portrait.

coached her on the answers to the questions, confident Philomena would learn to use her English effectively once she got the job. She was right. Philomena was hired, and soon she had not only learned how to be a librarian, but also received training to be a photo instructor.

Amberg

Philomena obtained the skills necessary to manage the photo lab in the Special Services Center of the U.S. Army base in Bayreuth. Later she was transferred to the photo lab of the Special Services Center at the U.S. Army base in Amberg, where she taught military personnel and their family members how to compose, take and process photographs. She also conducted photo tours of German cities and important historic places. She said the role of the Special Services Center was "to keep enlisted personnel and their dependents occupied and out of trouble."

John A. (for Augustus) Baker from Fort Kent, Maine, was one of the people who often visited the photo lab. Philomena was not interested in romance. She knew of relationships that had ended sadly for young German girls who fell in love with American soldiers. Nonetheless, John stood out. Their friendship grew after she was injured in an auto accident.

"I had exchanged my faithful bicycle, which had brought me to work and home again, for a small Lloyd car. On the day I received my driver's license, I decided to drive to Bayreuth where my mother lived and surprise her with my 'accomplishment.' It was June 6, 1958, my 24th birthday. It was a holiday for the Americans—D-Day—so I did not work that day.

"It was late afternoon. I was coming down a hill on a lightly traveled road. I noticed sparkles reflecting from broken glass on the pavement. I tried to avoid the glass, but it cut my tires and I swerved toward the right side of the road. The car flipped over three times as it rolled down a 12-foot embankment, throwing me out when the door on the driver's side flew open. I landed on

Philomena in her Special Services Photo Center uniform.

my stomach in a field of grass some 12 feet from the car. When I reached to adjust my wraparound skirt, I realized I could not move—my legs would not work. I tried to get up. I wanted to get closer to the road so I could wave someone down to help me. I could only move my arms, but they were not strong enough to pull my motionless body up the grass embankment.

"I had crawled closer to the road and was trying to pull myself up the steep bank with my hands and arms when a motorcyclist stopped. He told me not to move. There were no cell phones then, so he took off on his motorcycle for the nearest village to get an ambulance. In no time at all, the ambulance arrived and took me to a small hospital in a village a few kilometers away. There they took X-rays and determined that my pelvis was broken in three places and my hip was dislocated. They sent for another ambulance that took me to the hospital in Amberg, where I lived and worked at that time.

"When I awoke the next morning, I was in the hospital, my mother by my side and nurses tending to me. We learned that the broken glass in the road had come from a load of empty beer bottles that had spilled from the open back of a truck when it made a turn onto the road I was traveling.

"I was confined to the hospital for four months not knowing if I would ever walk again. Many of my photography students, their family members and enlisted people came to visit me. All of them gave me courage and the endurance to mend.

"One man never missed a day unless he was sent to patrol the border. On the first visit he brought me a tiny box of chocolates containing four candies. Each day he visited, he brought a larger box of candy until one day the gift was a five-pound box of chocolates, which was passed around to all the rooms on that floor of the hospital. This man impressed me. His name was Master Sergeant John A. Baker.

"He told me about the beauty of his home state of Maine and his life of fishing and hunting. He loved nature and described the brooks, the lakes, the trees and his work as a guide. Guests flew into his camps from everywhere in the United States to fish in the summer and hunt in the fall. He gave me a painting of a brook and woodland scene in Maine that is still displayed in my home. I didn't know if I would be able to walk again, but John didn't care. He wanted to marry me and proposed while I was still in the hospital."

Philomena became Mrs. John A. Baker on August 12, 1959. John was discharged October 3 of that year and seven weeks later Philomena said good-bye to her mother at the train station in Bayreuth and began her transatlantic journey to a new life in America. The train delivered her to Frankfurt where she boarded a military plane with other military personnel and dependents bound for New York City. There she transferred to a small plane that would take her to northern Maine where her new husband would be waiting to introduce her to a new home and a new family in Fort Kent.

Philomena and John Baker were married August 12, 1959, at the U.S. Army base in Amberg, Germany.

Philomena and John Baker celebrate their marriage with (from left) her cousin Viktoria with her husband and son; her mother, Philomene Keller, Father Beer, the priest who helped the family in Schwarzenbach, and his sister.

Philomene adjusts her daughter's bridal veil.

9

Maine

Family in Fort Kent

Philomena's first business in the United States on Main Street in
Fort Kent, Maine, (1960s).

"It was snowing when I got off the plane in Presque Isle. It was a late flight and it was dark outside. I was glad to be at my destination—calm and looking forward to seeing John. Time passed. He did not arrive. What could have detained him? There must be a good reason. It was not like John to be late. I knew he would be there one way or another, but I was all alone, not even an employee in sight. It might have been only half an hour, but it felt like eternity.

"Then John came through the door. I was sitting across the empty room. Was it really him? He smiled that familiar 'John smile.' For a moment we just stood and looked at each other.

When we embraced, reality struck and we didn't want to let go of each other."

John had been delayed after a hunter he was guiding shot a deer that had to be brought out of the woods to camp before he could leave for the airport. The Island Pond Camp, one of the old Red River camps owned by Herschel Curry, would be the newlyweds' home for the next three days. They arrived after midnight. Snow was falling lightly.

"The next day when I woke up, John was out on the lake with guests. I waited my turn to see him, but he was worth waiting for. He took me out on the lake and showed me the beauty that made him love northern Maine. It was hard for me to understand how they could make a sport of killing deer, though he tried to explain the importance of controlling the size of the herd. Eventually I came to understand their excitement for the sport, intellectually, if not emotionally. And I came to learn the importance of the guests and their wives."

Thanksgiving was a new holiday for Philomena. The only comparable holiday in Germany was a celebration of the harvest with an abundance of fruits and vegetables. The entire Baker family was waiting to meet her when she and John arrived in Fort Kent from the camp on November 27, 1959.

"You are my daughter and will always be my daughter," said John's mother Irene when she greeted Philomena. Everyone in John's family made her feel welcome: his parents Alton and Irene, and his siblings: Jesse, Eleanor, Hope, Joyce and Jim, and later on Don, who was living with his new wife and her family in Connecticut at the time.

"The next day the girls and I were peeling potatoes. Irene was making apple pies. They were setting a beautiful table, and I was part of it. It was wonderful. I could not have come to a better family. I had left my German family behind, but I now had brothers and sisters. We could not have loved each other more. We truly, truly accepted each other as siblings, and still do."

John Baker and his grandmother, Lily Baker, with her great-granddaughter, Deborah Bertha (for her godmother) Baker, born July 1, 1960.

John Baker at home on Eagle Lake in northern Maine.

Fort Kent Business and Professional Women President Philomena Baker (1967-1968) passes the gavel to incoming President Mary Sylvester.

John's father, Alton Baker, was the son of a veterinarian who had treated animals throughout Aroostook County. The Bakers were descendants of the patriot John Baker who gained fame for his Independence Day celebration on July 4, 1827, a time of dispute about which country would have control of the Upper St. John River Valley—Britain or the United States. Baker raised an American flag, made by his wife, on his land at the confluence of the St. John River and what is now Baker Brook. He declared the land to be in American territory. The New Brunswick attorney general disagreed. After an investigation and jury trial, Baker was fined 25 pounds for the act and jailed in Fredericton for two months, or until he could pay the fine.

It would be some time before Philomena learned this history behind her husband's name. The newlyweds lived in Fort Kent with John's family for a while, then were invited to move in with his grandmother, Lily Baker.

"Lily Baker lived in a big white house on Pleasant Street in Fort Kent. When John first introduced me to 'Memere Baker,' I fell in love with her immediately. Her sparkling blue eyes and her enchanting smile were surrounded by shining silver-gray hair that was loosely tied at the back of her head. I never knew any of my grandmothers personally, so this meeting was special."

John and his brother Donald were partners in their father's hardwood contracting business, Alton D. Baker & Sons. In the winter they cut wood. A Registered Maine Guide, John also operated the Camps of Acadia on Eagle Lake where he guided sportsmen on fishing and hunting excursions. When John was guiding or working in the woods, Philomena stayed with his grandmother.

"It was only natural for me to sense that Lily liked me, when she invited John and me to live with her. I was in good company with Memere Baker. She taught me how to prepare American meals, bake pies of all sorts and put the most delicious chowders and stews on the table with steaming bread and fresh butter.

Memere Baker taught me much more than how to prepare American meals. She taught me how to smile during that time, and how to serve meals with a happy attitude."

Professional Photography

Within two years, John and Philomena were the parents of two daughters, Deborah Bertha, born July 1, 1960, and Grace Rena Mae, born June 16, 1961. But parenting did not prevent Philomena from envisioning a photography business built on the skills she had acquired through the U.S. Army. She took every opportunity to enhance her training. She took courses in contemporary portrait photography at the University of New Hampshire, and received certificates of merit from the Winona School of Professional Portrait Photography in Indiana and the University of Maine Extension Service. She took many other courses offering her more opportunities to grow professionally, especially when black-and-white photography gave way to color.

Philomena and John eventually made their home at 64 Main Street in the middle of Fort Kent. They converted the front sections of their first floor into a reception and sales area, photographic studio and darkroom facility. They lived in an apartment behind the business in the same building. Philomena cashed in her U.S. Army retirement early in order to purchase the equipment she needed, and took the bus to Boston to pick up her new professional photo equipment.

After two years of planning and preparation she opened Baker Studio specializing in fine portraiture, weddings, receptions and commercial photography. The studio gained such an excellent reputation for weddings that Philomena would sometimes be asked to photograph two or three ceremonies on the same day. Couples would time their weddings so she could cover them all.

"I would photograph the bride and groom separately at their homes or at the church preparing for the wedding. Then

I photographed the guests and family members arriving at the church. I stayed at the church until the exchange of rings. Then I took the 4-by-5 negatives to the studio where John processed the film and printed the proofs in time for me to display them at the reception so the guests could select and place their orders.

"Then I went back to the church, photographed the newlyweds coming out and followed them to the reception, usually held at the local armory, the hotel or other reception facility. Many guests came from out of town and out of state and were very happy to see the proofs and place their orders at that time."

When she had taken the prescribed photos at the reception, she moved on to the next wedding where the procedure was repeated. "It always worked out," she said, admitting that the Fort Kent police chief might still remember stopping her on occasion as she sped from one place to another.

Philomena competed successfully with nationally known Stevens Studio of Bangor for the contract to photograph high school graduates in Fort Kent. With her innate eye for color she hand tinted black-and-white portraits in the years before color film was available.

Under her leadership, the local Business and Professional Women's organization grew from 30 to 103 members. This group mailed some 30 care packages to local military men serving in Vietnam. As charter president of the Fort Kent "Dollars for Scholars" program, Philomena helped local high school students attend college by organizing rummage sales and setting up "coffee corners" to collect donations.

"I loved the people in Fort Kent. They were my extended family. I felt as though I had always lived there." Many Fort Kent residents visited Philomena after her marriage ended in divorce and she moved to Hampden in 1970 with her two daughters. She worked with Stevens Studios for two years then opened her own studio in Hampden. She grew her business into one of the largest studios and color processing labs in New England. Employing as many as 12 people at times, Baker Color Lab pioneered color processing and printing for in- and out-of-state professional photographers.

"Other photographers said they would never change from black-and-white to color, but I was drawn to color. The film and my Hasselblad camera were lighter in weight than the heavy 4-by-5 professional cameras we used until the early 1970s. I said 'good-bye' to black-and-white, and changed to color."

Last memories

Philomena's sensitivity to color was evident even when she was a child. The reader may remember that, as she boarded the box-car to leave her home in Odessa forever, she was mesmerized by the golden shades of the setting sun and resolved to "always remember these varying shades of gold." And at age 78, she still remembered that on the day she and her mother began their long walk through Germany in 1945, "the apple trees were dressed with beautiful blossoms."

Philomena's appreciation of photography has deep roots. She can identify her ancestors because they hired a professional photographer to document important occasions and family gatherings, such as a 50th anniversary celebration in 1908. When her mother, Philomene, knew her loved ones were threatened by illness or war, she arranged to have them photographed. When forced to leave her home with only the things she could carry, her mother chose to carry her family photographs. And when she knew those photos might be damaged or lost during her treacherous walk to freedom, she entrusted them to a young farm wife who had given her and her daughter shelter.

After Philomena and her mother were safe and settled at the Behelfsheim in Bayreuth, and when civilians were once again allowed to travel by train, Philomene made the promised trip back into Russian-occupied Germany to recover the photos she had left at the farm near Potsdam. She called upon Viktoria to care for Philomena while she was gone.

It was the season for harvest and Philomene hoped she would find some apples to bring home to her family. Apples were so precious they were saved until Christmas to use as tree decorations. When she returned, she had not only the package of photographs and documents, but also a special treat—apples.

Long after Philomene had died, Philomena learned from Viktoria that her mother had found more than photographs and apples on this trip. She had learned through the Red Cross about a Russian encampment located near Potsdam. Perhaps her husband, Philomena's father, might be there. She decided she would try to locate the camp while she was in the area. It was out of the way, but Philomene found it and located an office. She asked about her husband.

"Yes, we have a Semenenko—Wasja Semenenko."

Her spirit must have soared as the office manager pointed to a building among the barracks.

"That's where he is living with his family."

Stunned, Philomene thanked him and moved away. She stood out of sight of the building. Could it be him? Did she want to see him ... them? Could she bear to disturb a family?

No. She could not. She would believe he was alive. That was all she needed.

"She never told me," said Philomena. "She felt the heartache and did not want me to experience the pain."

Philomene would be content with the good fortune that had kept her and her daughter alive and together through their long journey to freedom. She would just remember Wasja. She had his photograph.

Epilogue
The Race Walker

Full Circle

At age 56, Philomena won the gold medal in the
10,000-meter racewalk at the 1990 U.S. National
Masters' racewalking competition at the Purdue Sport
Complex in Indianapolis, Indiana.

In the 1980s and 1990s, Philomena's personal history as a citizen
of Russia, Germany and the United States resurfaced when she
gained international recognition as a racewalker. A sport with
Olympic status in Europe, racewalking was yet to become popular in the United States.

So when Philomena and her then husband and coach Dr.
Moshe Myerowitz of Bangor, Maine, entered an international

competition in Turku, Finland, in 1991, they were dark horses. Their rivals from around the world were former Olympians.

At age 56, Philomena had won the gold in her category for the 10,000-meter race at the 1990 National Masters' Racewalking Competition held at the Purdue Sports Complex in Indianapolis, Indiana. Her achievement caught the eye of *Sports Illustrated* magazine, which named her one of four "Faces in the Crowd," the only one of the four with masters' status. Still, the Europeans had no statistics comparable to those of athletes from other nations.

When she and Myerowitz arrived in Turku, she was able to converse with Russian team members in their own language. It was the first year Russia had competed in the international races, and the government was concerned about defections. Team members did not have the freedom of movement other athletes enjoyed, but were always transported from place to place as a group on a bus. During the competition in Turku, they stayed on a ship where some of them slept on tables.

As competitors assembled at the stadium, Philomena chatted with the top Russian racewalker asking about her times.

"She told me she didn't know her exact times because only the coach was allowed to have a watch. I took off my watch and gave it to her so she could know her times. I noticed her shoes were worn out. She told me those were the only ones she had."

Nonetheless, the Russian woman won the 10,000-meter race. Baker placed second and the third place winner was a German.

"All three of my nationalities were standing on that podium. I represented the United States, but each national anthem stirred something inside me."

As the Russian winner rose to her place on the top step of the podium, Philomena noticed she was wearing the watch. Little did the Russian champion know that while the world was honoring her victory, the bus carrying her team back to the ship was leaving the stadium without her. "She was frantic. I was the only one she could talk to," said Philomena. "We invited her to ride on the bus carrying American and German teams to their hotel. She sat stiff, fearful. I tried to comfort her, assuring her she was not to blame for missing her bus. When our bus arrived, two coaches were waiting for her and whisked her back to the ship."

From the international competition in Finland, Philomena and her husband traveled to Baden, Switzerland, for the European Masters' Championships. Just before the 5,000-meter race, Philomena overheard members of the German team in the women's restroom talking to each other about the upcoming competition.

"I heard them say, in German, 'We have to do our very best to beat the Americans.' Hearing my own language, I identified with them, telling myself I would have to do my very best. Then I looked down at my uniform and realized they were talking about me. I was the American. That just intensified my determination to win that 5,000-meter race for the Americans."

And she did, the first American woman to take a gold medal in the European Masters' racewalking competition. Unaware that Philomena was of German descent, her German rivals could not have known, as she stepped to the top of the podium, that *they* had provided the extra incentive for her to win.

And few people realized that Philomena's strength as a racewalker was a natural evolution for a person who had walked halfway across Germany at the age of 10.

Sports Illustrated magazine named Philomena one of four "Faces in the Crowd" after she placed first in the 1990 U.S. Masters' racewalk competition. Joe McLaughlin, then assistant sports editor of the *Bangor Daily News,* presented her with the trophy on behalf of the magazine. (*Bangor Daily News* photo).

Afterword

How life evolved

Philomene Keller remained in Bayreuth, where she worked initially at the U.S. Army base. She visited her daughter in Fort Kent and later moved to New York City, where she lived and worked for several years at a Catholic residence for retired women. Then she returned to Bayreuth and lived in a retirement home until her death on July 9, 1992, at age 88.

Julia Hartmann and her family moved to the Bonn area after the war where she took care of the family home.

Angelika, now deceased, became the secretary to the head surgeon of a hospital in Bonn and, after retirement, cared for her mother, Julia, until her death at 98 years of age.

Viktoria became a pharmacist after obtaining the necessary training at the Bayreuth U.S. Army base. She and her husband have two grown children and live in Germany.

Alfred became a master tailor, specializing in suits and uniforms. He and his wife have two daughters and live in Germany.

Johannes lives in Germany where he retired in the early 2000s from a career as a restorer of cathedrals. He and his wife have three children, two of whom also became restorers.

John A. Baker was a Registered Maine Guide for hunters and fishermen and owner of Camps of Acadia on Eagle Lake in northern Maine. He died in Bangor July 2, 1991.

Deborah Baker became a chiropractor with a practice in Hampden, Maine, where she lives with her two sons.

Grace Baker Cater became a chiropractor and practices in Boston, Massachusetts, where she lives with her husband Ronald Cater.

Philomena and her two daughters, Deborah and Grace (center), in Germany in 1979 with her cousin Alfred Hartmann (right), his mother, Julia Hartmann and his wife, Anneliese (seated), and their two daughters, Julia Agnes (left) and Regina (center).

Julia Hartmann and her sons, Johannes (standing) and Alfred, in Germany, 1979.

Philomena's daughters, Deborah and Grace, with their great-aunt Julia in Germany, 1979.

Philomene Keller moved to New York City where she worked in a retirement home for Catholic women before returning to Bayreuth where she died in 1992.

Philomena Baker photographed generations of Maine families during her 40-year career in portraiture, as is evident in this wall of portraits displayed at the Bangor Auditorium in the 1970s.

Philomena received national and regional awards for her portrait photography between the 1970s and 1990s. Here she displays the Best of Show trophy awarded by the Maine Professional Photographers Association in 1977.

Sources

Bach, Julian Jr. *America's Germany, An Account of the Occupation*. New York: Random House, 1946.

Cawthorne, Nigel. *The Story of the SS: Hitler's Infamous Legions of Death*. New York: Chartwell Books, Inc., 2011.

Craig, Gordon A. *Europe Since 1815*. New York: Holt, Rinehart and Winston, Inc., 1961.

Dollinger, Hans. *The Decline and Fall of Nazi Germany and Imperial Japan: A Pictorial History of the Final Days of World War II*. Translated from the German by Arnold Pomerans; technical adviser, Dr. Hans-Adolf Jacobsen. New York: Bonanza Books, 1965.

Frazier, Ian. "On the Prison Highway: the gulag's silent remains." *The New Yorker*, Aug. 30, 2010, pp. 28 –34.

Gilbert, Martin. *The Routledge Atlas of the Holocaust*. Third Edition. London: Routledge Publishing, 2002.

----- . *The Second World War: A Complete History*. New York: Henry Holt & Company, 1989, Reissued 2004.

Heinrich, Bernd. *The Snoring Bird: My Family's Journey through a Century of Biology*. New York: Harper Collins Publishers, 2007.

Magosci, Paul Robert. *Ukraine: An Illustrated History*. Seattle: University of Washington Press, 2007.

Mahoney, Kevin, ed. *In Pursuit of Justice: Examining the Evidence of the Holocaust*. Washington, D.C.: United States Holocaust Memorial Museum, 1996.

Moorehead, Alan. *The Russian Revolution*. New York: Harper Brothers Publishers, 1958.

Owings, Alison. *Frauen: German Women Recall the Third Reich.* New Brunswick, N.J.: Rutgers University Press, 1995.

Ray, John. *The Illustrated History of World War II.* London: Weidenfeld & Nicolson, The Orion Publishing Group, Ltd., 2003.

Rubenstein, Joshua, and Ilya Altman, eds. *The Unknown Black Book: The Holocaust in The German-Occupied Soviet Territories.* United States Holocaust Memorial Museum and Indiana University Press, 2008.

*Schmaltz, Eric J. "Clothed with the Dead: Directives from Himmler to Pohl and Lorenz, 24 October 1942, concerning the Delivery to Ethnic Germans of Consignments of Clothing from Lublin and Auschwitz Warehouses," *Heritage Review* (Germans from Russia Heritage Society), Vol. 42, No. 4 (December 2012): pp. 12-13.

Sulzberger, C. L. *The American Heritage Picture History of World War II.* American Heritage Publishing Co., 1966.

Time-Life Books. *WWII: Time-Life Books History of the Second World War.* New York: Prentice-Hall Press, 1989.

*Vossler, Ronald. *Flaming Ovens: The Untold Story of Hitler's Steppe-Children and the Holocaust's Bloodiest Genocidaires* (tentative title). To be published by Germans from Russia Heritage Collection, North Dakota State University Libraries.

---

* Schmaltz and Vossler have documented that clothing of Jewish people murdered by Nazis in death camps in occupied Poland and by German police under SS command in open killings across Ukraine was distributed to ethnic Germans in Odessa and elsewhere by an ethnic German liaison office during the German occupation of the Soviet Union.

Acknowledgements

The authors are grateful to the numerous people who contributed to the creation of *Flight to Freedom*, and to the *Bangor Daily News* for previewing it as a seven-part series in 2010, in print and on the web. Joni Dunn at Bangor Photo scanned all the photos onto CDs, and Steve and Mattie at Java Joe's in Bangor always had a table available for Philomena and Kathryn to spend hours discussing the manuscript. Sincere thanks to those who read and in some cases re-read the manuscript several times: Michael Alpert, David Bergquist, Marc Berlin, Kristine Bondeson, Ardeana Hamlin, Robert Klose, Lucy Leaf, Rick Levasseur, Nancy MacKnight, Dorothy McDuffie, Mary-Ann McHugh, Dr. Moshe Myerowitz, Christopher Peary, Anette Ruppel Rodrigues, Scott Ruffner, Glenna Johnson Smith and Susan Wold; and to those who gave other kinds of encouragement and information: Dr. Deborah Baker, Donald Baker, John Branson, Alfred Hartmann, Johannes Hartmann, Viktoria Hartmann, Marquita Hill, Thomas Morelli, Deanna Partridge, Eric Schmaltz and Ronald Vossler.

All Keller and Hartmann family photographs are provided by Philomena Baker.

Gratitude

Throughout my life, I felt I had an, oh, so important story to tell of "war through the eyes of a child." With all of its twists and turns, my life was filled with blessings every step of the way. One of those blessings came when writer and author Kathryn Olmstead entered my life. She graciously accepted my offer to help me fulfill my dream of putting my memories of living through war as a child on paper. Her eloquence, persistence and unwavering encouragement resulted in this personal history that has captured the heart and soul of my life and that of many others.

Philomena Keller Baker
October 2012

About The Authors

Philomena Keller Baker
Portrait by Thomas Morelli

Philomena Baker was born in Odessa, Ukraine, June 6, 1934, the only child of a Russian father and German mother. In 1944, she was evacuated with her mother and relatives in one of two boxcars for German civilians attached to a hospital train of wounded German soldiers. They received German citizenship papers upon entry into German-occupied Poland. After her flight to freedom described on these pages, she lived in the American sector of occupied Germany, wherein she received her education. She was subsequently employed as a photo instructor for servicemen and their dependents in the Special Services Division at the U.S. Army Base in Amberg, Germany. In 1959, she married MSgt. John A. Baker in Amberg and immigrated to Fort Kent, Maine, where they became the parents of two daughters, Deborah Bertha and Grace Rena Mae, and where she founded Baker Studio specializing in fine portraiture. Philomena became a U.S. citizen December 4, 1968. After her marriage ended in divorce in 1970, she and her daughters moved to Hampden, where she opened a photographic studio that became well known for fine portraiture and for graduation photographs that drew contracts from high schools and colleges throughout the Northeast. In 1987 she married Bangor chiropractor Dr. Moshe Myerowitz, who also became her coach for racewalking. They competed nationally and internationally and she became a champion, as described in the Epilogue. She closed her photography business in the 1990s in order to pursue the practice of Reiki, a hands-on healing system founded by Usui Sensei (1865-1927) in Japan. She became a Reiki master and teacher, fifth in the lineage originated by Usui, and opened the Bangor Reiki Center in 1997.

Kathryn Olmstead
Photograph by Michael Gudreau

Kathryn Olmstead is a columnist for the *Bangor Daily News*, free-lance writer and editor/publisher of *Echoes* magazine, a quarterly journal of rural culture based in Caribou, Maine, which she co-founded in 1988. She served 25 years on the journalism faculty of the University of Maine in Orono, the last six years as associate dean in the College of Liberal Arts and Sciences. Formerly she was a correspondent for the *Bangor Daily News*, editor of the *Aroostook Republican* weekly newspaper in Caribou, free-lance agricultural journalist for regional and national newspapers in Vermont and Kansas, and regional representative for U.S. Senator Bill Cohen. A native of Battle Creek, Michigan, she earned a bachelor of arts in English from the University of Illinois, Champaign-Urbana, and a master of arts in English and education from the University of Wisconsin, Madison. She taught English at Wauwatosa East High School in Wisconsin and English and journalism at Concord High School in New Hampshire before moving to Maine in 1974.